THINK HOMESCHOOL©
· live & learn your way™ ·

A HomeSchool ThinkTank™ Book
Book One

THINK HOMESCHOOL
• live & learn your way •

A HomeSchool ThinkTank™ Book
Book One

JACKIE WHEELER

Cover and Interior Design by
Monica Woodward, iDesign

Edited by J.S. Avis

HSTT Press
An Imprint of HomeSchool ThinkTank™ LLC

Copyright © 2018 Jackie Wheeler. All rights reserved.
No part of this book may be reproduced, distributed, or transmitted in any form or by any means, including photocopying, recording, or other electronic or mechanical methods, without prior written permission from the publisher, except in the case of brief quotations embodied in critical reviews and for certain other noncommercial uses permitted by the United States of America copyright law. For permission request, email the publisher through www.homeschoolthinktank.com. Use the words "permission request" in the subject line. HomeSchool ThinkTank™, LLC; P.O. Box 6107; Farmington, NM 87499

Library of Congress Control Number: 2018950750

The information presented herein represents the view of the author as of the date of first publication. This book is presented for informational purposes only. The author reserves the right to alter and update her opinions at any time. Although the author and publisher have made every effort to ensure that the information in this book was correct on the date of first publication, the publisher and its affiliates, partners, and authors do not assume and do hereby disclaim any liability for loss, damage, or disruption caused by reliance on this book or the information contained herein, including any inaccuracies, errors, or omissions. Portions of this book are works of nonfiction. Certain names and identifying characteristics may have been changed. Names that have not been changed have been used with consent. Information and links to www.homeschoolthinktank.com and other organizations are provided solely for the reader's benefit and do not reflect any past or present business relationship between the author, the publisher, and any third parties. Reference to another organization does not positively or negatively indicate its affiliation with HomeSchool ThinkTank™, LLC or the author. HomeSchool ThinkTank™, LLC, its owners, partners, authors, or affiliates do not presume to give legal or other professional advice and specifically disclaim any liability, loss, or risk, personal or otherwise, that is incurred as a consequence, directly or indirectly, of the use and application of any of the contents of this book or other associated books, websites, social media platforms, podcasts, video, or public speaking events.

Trademark Notice:
Application has been filed with the USPTO for HomeSchool ThinkTank™, live & learn your way,™ and the HomeSchool ThinkTank™, LLC logo that is seen below. At the time of first printing, these are unregistered trademarks.

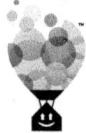

Text by Jackie Wheeler
Cover and Interior Design by Monica Woodward, iDesign
Cover Photo of Author used with permission; © Mandy Walters 2018
Interior Photo of Author used with permission; © Jeffrey Pierson Studio 2018

Published by

HSTT Press,
an imprint of HomeSchool ThinkTank™, LLC.

Publisher's Cataloging-in-Publication Data
provided by Five Rainbows Cataloging Services

Names: Wheeler, Jackie Michelle, author.
Title: Think homeschool : live & learn your way / by Jackie Wheeler.
Description: First edition. | Farmington, NM : HomeSchool ThinkTank, 2018. | Series: A HomeSchool ThinkTank book.
Identifiers: LCCN 2018950750 | ISBN 978-1-949377-00-2 (hardcover) | ISBN 978-1-949377-01-9 (pbk.) | ISBN 978-1-949377-02-6 (ebook) | 978-1-949377-03-3 (audiobook)
Subjects: LCSH: Home schooling--Handbooks, manuals, etc. | Home schooling--Social aspects. | Education--Parent participation. | Learning. | Academic achievement. | BISAC: EDUCATION / Home Schooling. | EDUCATION / Parent Participation. | FAMILY & RELATIONSHIPS / Education. | FAMILY & RELATIONSHIPS / Life Stages / School Age.
Classification: LCC LC40 .W51 2018 (print) | LCC LC40 (ebook) | DDC 371.04/2--dc23.

Printed in the United States of America.
First Edition, 2018.

*To my children,
for teaching me
the lessons that
I could only learn
from you.*

THINK HOMESCHOOL

TABLE OF CONTENTS

- A Pertinent Preface 13
- Itty Bitty Introduction 17
- Part I: Kindred Goals 19
- Part II: Homeschool Living 23
- Part III: Homeschool Opportunities 35
- Part IV: Homeschool Routines 39
- Part V: Homeschool Hurdles 45
- Part VI: Homeschool Laws and More 53
- Part VII: Homeschool Hopefully 57
- Part VIII: Encouraging Epilogue 63
- Notable Acknowledgements 67
- About the Author 70
- HomeSchool ThinkTank™ Happenings! 71

A HomeSchool ThinkTank™ Book
Book One

A PERTINENT PREFACE

2017 SCHOOL SHOOTING

It was my birthday, and I was looking forward to it. I was eating breakfast with my family and visiting about the upcoming day. My children were getting ready to participate in a homeschool talent show that afternoon.

The text came out of the blue.

There was a shooting at a local high school.

Just minutes before, my mother–a bus driver for that same school district–was pulling away from the high school. She was oblivious to what was already beginning. Not long after my mom left, sirens screamed by, and a call came over the radio notifying the bus drivers to keep their distance from the school. That day–like any other day–my mother had dropped high school students off for a day at school. On that morning, evil walked amongst the students. Only the shooter knew of the dreadful things that would happen that day.

I thought of my mom, wondering if she was okay. My brother lives nearby. Would this impact him? I know children who attend that school. My heart sank; my stomach churned. As the implications sunk in, I cried. I learned people had died; I felt like vomiting. The entire town was locking down. My oldest daughter's friend heard the gunshots. My younger daughter's dear friend huddled in a closet, at a nearby middle school, and trembled in fear with classmates. Terrified children were calling their parents with heartbreaking words: "I might die today, and I want you to know I love you."

Two teenagers died before the shooter killed himself.

A Week Later…

My friend comes to me; she is considering homeschooling her youngest daughter. The family had thought about homeschooling before the school year began. Now, after the shooting, she is considering homeschooling again. The mother doesn't want to send her oldest child either, but he is a senior within months of graduating.

The first week students resume school, my friend doesn't send either child back. The second week, both of her children return to school. As I reflect on our conversations, I realize that I have not adequately expressed what homeschooling really is. I wish I could take the unknown out of homeschooling. I want to convey how homeschooling is about education *and* life. I decide to write this book for her. I decide to write this book for the world. People *need* this book.

THINK HOMESCHOOL

On that fateful day, book writing was already on my mind. I was inspired by my thirteen-year-old daughter, who started writing novels over two years ago. She was finally getting close to finishing one and wanted to publish it. To help my daughter, I needed to learn the process. Since I have a wealth of knowledge and experience around homeschooling, I had already chosen that as my topic. However, I never dreamed that such a dreadful thing would become the catalyst for my first book.

Over the years, many people have asked me about homeschooling. Sometimes they are mothers of young children; sometimes they are parents who are unhappy with the school system. Occasionally, people just seem curious. However, this is the only time someone has asked me about homeschooling in a situation like this. Tragically, violence in schools seems to be more common than ever. As a result, even more parents are choosing to homeschool their children.

Since our community's school shooting, several local families have turned to homeschooling. To be clear, I am not suggesting that people live their lives in fear. We all know that anything can happen anywhere. However, when terrible things happen, I think it is completely reasonable that parents would want to pull their children out of school and that children wouldn't want to go back to school. As I hear stories in my community, I wonder if returning to school is healthy? If something terrible happened to you, would you want to return to the place where the dreadful thing happened, day after day? I am not a psychologist; I have not been in that situation and cannot speak to it. This is just what I wonder.

ITTY BITTY INTRODUCTION

Homeschooling is an amazing opportunity. I am grateful for the freedom to homeschool my children and for organizations who continuously fight to protect that freedom.

Throughout this book, I want to share many thoughts with you. I want to take the unknown out of homeschooling. You will see why homeschooling is an outstanding opportunity and how it can help your children and family thrive. You will realize that homeschooling doesn't have to be expensive, and it isn't as daunting as many think. You will envision how you can homeschool your children and how there are many ways to educate them. You will understand how homeschoolers educate their children from home and in their community as well. You will begin to see how homeschool families can engage in a variety of meaningful relationships and lead a fulfilling life. Hopefully, you will appreciate that homeschooling is not just about education, but about a lifestyle.

THINK HOMESCHOOL.

Homeschooling is an experience that can enrich your entire family's life. Homeschoolers are out in the world and learning every day. Education doesn't only happen in workbooks or on a computer. *Life* is education. Hopefully, you will see how you really can *Live & Learn Your Way.*™

Live & Learn Your Way™
HOMESCHOOL THINKTANK™

HomeSchool ThinkTank™ connects homeschool families with one another and the resources we need.

PART I

KINDRED GOALS

We have children and want to raise them well. We want to enjoy spending time with our kids, but how much time do most of us have with our children? When your child was in the womb, did you dream of dropping your kids off five days a week? Did you imagine picking them up between three and six o'clock every night? Were you looking forward to spending their school years rushing from one activity to the next? Are you excited to stay up late helping with homework assignments? When people say, "I want to have a baby," do you think they are looking that far down the road? It seems unlikely.

When we have children, we should become intentional about structuring our family, raising our kids, and the outcomes that are best for our individual children and family. As you consider homeschooling, here are some questions you might ask yourself. Think about them, and answer yourself honestly.

THINK HOMESCHOOL

- How much family time do you want, and how do you see your family spending that time?

- What level of education do you want for your children?

- Does your child's school provide the education you desire?

- Would your child benefit from education you could provide through homeschooling that is not offered through the school system?

- Are your children learning things at school that you would prefer they didn't learn?

- How do you think your child learns best?

- How can you help your children develop a good work ethic?

- How can you raise your children to care about themselves, their family, and community?

- Do your children have good relationships with family and friends?

- Do your children need flexibility in scheduling to pursue activities they are passionate about?

- How do you think your schedule would look if your children homeschooled?

- Is your child mentally healthy?

- Is your child active and physically fit?

- Is your child happy?

THINK HOMESCHOOL

- Are you living the lifestyle you want to live?

- Finally, if you homeschooled your children, could your family *Live & Learn Your Way*™?

As you answer these questions about your family, consider that we want to raise children who are caring, intelligent, and responsible. We want our children to be physically, emotionally, intellectually, and spiritually healthy. So, is homeschooling the best way to help your family thrive? That's a question for you to answer, but we can help you envision how homeschooling could be right for your family. This book will help you see that you are capable of homeschooling your own children. If you think homeschooling is the answer for your family, you will feel empowered to move forward and begin your homeschooling journey.

Throughout this book, please think about your goals for your family and children. Consider the best way to help your family live the life you desire, and the best way to help your children become adults who fulfill their potential and live the life they yearn for. Regardless of how your children are educated, parental involvement is key. However, we believe homeschooling provides opportunities and benefits that every family should be aware of and consider.

As parents, we would be delighted to see our children grow up to become happy adults. We are pleased to see our adult children become productive citizens in society who do good in the world. Wouldn't it be great if your kids could do that *and* live life on their terms? The question is, "How do you get there?" We will show how homeschooling can help your children and family *Live & Learn Your Way*.™

HomeSchool ThinkTank™
• live & learn your way™ •

"We believe homeschooling provides opportunities and benefits that every family should be aware of and consider."
HOMESCHOOL THINKTANK™

PART II

HOMESCHOOL LIVING

What is homeschooling? Homeschooling is living and learning your way, on your terms. Homeschooling is not only about the child but about the entire family. Homeschooling is a lifestyle. Sure, we use workbooks and computer programs to teach academic foundations, but we are quick to expand upon the many other lessons life has to offer. Homeschoolers understand that school and a solid academic education are not necessarily synonymous. We see that the education a child receives in school is not necessarily the education parents have in mind for their children. We feel there is so much more to teach a child than schools can or should teach. Homeschoolers realize that a complete education involves far more than academics. We feel that children should expand their knowledge from home with more parental guidance than the school system allows.

THINK HOMESCHOOL

Who Homeschools...

All types of people homeschool. Our kids are already signed up in afterschool activities with your kids. We shop where you shop, and when you visit with us, you might not have any idea we homeschool our children. Homeschoolers are out and about, living and learning in the world, every day. Education happens not only from home but through volunteer opportunities, at the library, the museum, the nature center, and with other kids who homeschool. Homeschoolers have rich and varied friendships and participate in a myriad of activities. We are out in the world, just like you.

> *"Homeschoolers have rich and varied friendships and participate in a myriad of activities."*
> **HOMESCHOOL THINKTANK™**

The Homeschool Lifestyle...

First and foremost, homeschooling is a lifestyle. Homeschooling effects more than the children; it impacts the entire family dynamic. Yes, homeschooling is about education, but it involves much more than dedicated academic materials. When a family chooses to homeschool, and one parent stays home with the kids, life is altered drastically. Homeschool families set their own schedule and teach their children in a way that works best for each child, *and* in a way that works for the family as well. If you know five homeschooling families, it is quite likely that each family not only has very different schedules, but they also educate their children differently from one another as well. Ultimately, homeschooling impacts the entire family, and each family lives and learns in their own way.

Homeschool Families...

Homeschooling is good for families. School and homework can interfere with family time greatly. When we homeschool, there isn't necessarily homework. While homeschool kids may choose to do schoolwork in the evening, the key word is *choose*. While it is always an option to work on academic areas, if the family prefers to spend time in other ways, we have a choice. Each homeschooling family lives and learns differently. The bottom line is we do what works for our specific family. Homeschool families balance academics and life as needed. On the other hand, school families live their lives by the school's schedule.

Homeschooling and Values...

As homeschooling parents, we have more time with our children. With this time, we have an increased opportunity to share morals and lifestyle values. Also, it is easier for homeschool parents to help guide our children's friendships by increasing time with kids and families we think well of. Finally, we can guide other activities and experiences to help form our children well. People of all ages tend to become like those they associate with, so it is important to surround your family with people you admire.

THINK HOMESCHOOL

As our children get older and have varied life experiences, there will be an increasing number of opportunities for important conversations. Once again, for homeschool families, time is on our side. With hours spent together, we can help impart our views, and our children can share their perspective. These discussions can create excellent critical thinking skills. Our children will grow up, have their own viewpoint and live their life as they wish. However, while they live at home, we can help share the life values we hope our children will adopt.

> *"As homeschooling parents, we have more time with our children. With this time, we have an increased opportunity to share morals and lifestyle values."*
> **HOMESCHOOL THINKTANK™**

Homeschooling and Life…

Homeschool families have more flexible time in their schedule than public school families. The typical child spends approximately 38 hours per week at school. Unfortunately, school kids still come home with approximately 5-15 hours a week of homework. On top of that, add the time kids are commuting back and forth to school. Finally, if your kids are involved with other after-school options, then you can probably add another 3-20 hours a week for those activities. After a full week of school, homework, and school-related activities, there isn't much time for family and life outside of school.

THINK HOMESCHOOL

While the average school child spends approximately 38 hours per week at school, many states base a homeschool week on 30 hours a week. So why is there such a discrepancy? The amount of time wasted in school is great. Consider the time spent on classroom management, calling roll, standing in line, and changing subjects. Then there's lunch and recess, and while these are necessary breaks, this isn't academic time. Finally, the amount of unfocused and interrupted time adds up, and the result is homework. So even after spending nearly 8 hours a day at school, children are still expected to come home and do more schoolwork. The homeschooled child, on the other hand, can learn the lesson, then complete the task at hand. They can do this at their own pace–in one sitting or until a break is needed.

Now, when you consider you are likely spending around two hours a day transporting your kids to school and helping them with homework, why not consider homeschooling? You have already given your kids a significant amount of time that it takes to complete a homeschool day. As for your kids, they will enjoy having more time to *Live & Learn Your Way.*™

Homeschooling and Flexibility...

While educating children is essential, doing things as they are done in public school isn't. When local law allows, it is more practical to be flexible. When homeschooled children are involved in activities where practices are more time-consuming at various times of the year, then consider adjusting the schedule accordingly. For instance, a homeschool student might lighten their academic workload when they are very busy with an activity. Once the activity slows down, then the academic workload can be increased again. Likewise, if your children do activities that are dependent on specific weather, schedule around it; this can be done seasonally or daily.

THINK HOMESCHOOL

One extreme but useful example is snowboarding. Practice times for snowboarding do not go well with a traditional school schedule. Not only is the prime season in the winter, but good snowboarding hours might be from 10:00 a.m. to 3:00 p.m. In this instance, the student could still work on other academic areas in the early morning or evening. Maybe a lesson of math could be completed before hitting the slopes. Later, after dinner, the student could read, do art, write, or watch educational documentaries and videos. Once the snowboarding season is over, the homeschool student could increase their academic workload again. A homeschool student can hustle to have the summer off with other school kids, or they can decide to school year-round. If your local law allows, they might even choose to take the traditional long break in the winter as opposed to the summer. The flexibility of homeschooling allows families to live and learn on their terms. This is how HomeSchool ThinkTank™ coined the term *Live & Learn Your Way.*™

While it is important to follow your local laws, homeschoolers can frequently choose when to do schoolwork. When necessary or desired, homeschool students can follow the traditional school calendar and complete around 6 hours of schoolwork each school day. On the other hand, many homeschoolers choose alternative schedules. For example, if we choose to do school nearly year-round 48 weeks of the year, then our kids need to do about 4.5 hours per school day of dedicated schoolwork 5 days per week. Consider, this does not all have to be math books and grammar. There's reading, physical education, music, history, science, and more. In addition, you may be surprised at how much educational value life has to offer outside of your core curriculum. Ultimately, when we embrace the flexibility of homeschooling and embody life as education, we find that most of our days become one fluid part of our children's education. The outcome can be a child who is a self-motivated, lifelong learner. What more could a teacher ask for?

THINK HOMESCHOOL

Homeschooling Isn't Public School...

Yes, some families try to emulate the public school schedule. However, this schedule isn't ideal for many homeschool families. Likewise, it's not ideal for schools either. If the school schedule and environment were ideal, school children would come home with their evenings free, not homework.

Instead of trying to imitate public schools, homeschoolers might consider educating their children in a way that works best for their child and family. When parents try to re-create the public school system in the home, it can be exhausting and frustrating for the entire family. We are not suggesting you neglect your child's education. We are asking you to consider other ways to educate your children that might be more realistic, more effective, and have better outcomes for both your children and family. We will introduce a few ideas in the following chapters.

> *"We are asking you to consider other ways to educate your children that might be more realistic, more effective, and have better outcomes for both your children and family."*
> **HOMESCHOOL THINKTANK™**

THINK HOMESCHOOL

Individualizing Homeschooling...

Homeschool families have educational decisions to make. Think about how your child learns best. As you try different approaches, realize that a learning curve is inevitable. Consider choosing curriculum for one subject area and introducing it. After implementing, then order and begin working with the next piece of curriculum. It is easy to be overzealous and think we can do more than is realistic. Sometimes, education is more effective when we take a nontraditional approach. For example, instead of reading history textbooks, maybe audiobooks, documentaries, or biographies are a better option. Likewise, science projects and videos might be more effective than reading from a textbook. If we want our children to become avid readers, it is best to make reading as enjoyable as possible. As for writing, we want our children to practice, but few children have the patience to sit at a table for hours on end. At the very least, consider breaking up writing assignments with other activities. It is a good idea to mix up the ways we help our children learn. Here are some other ideas to consider:

- The relationship with our children is more important than *school*. If life and homeschooling are less than pleasant, then we should reconsider how we are educating our children and structuring our day.

- As a parent and teacher, instilling the love of learning is far more important than any curriculum. Yes, learning can be work. However, it should be more pleasant than frustrating. Children who love to learn will pursue education even when they aren't directed to.

THINK HOMESCHOOL

- Does your child learn best by watching, listening, talking, writing, moving, doing, or feeling? Consider mixing educational methods; this makes homeschooling more fun, increases retention, and reduces boredom with learning.

- Preview curriculum. To view curriculum, attend a homeschool convention, ask to see another homeschooler's curriculum, and check materials out from the library. Always look at the table of contents and sample pages offered by online providers.

- Consider your child's personality and your own. Some methods and curriculum may be more effective than others for your family. How well you and your child communicate does matter. When needed, it is possible to minimize your involvement. Parents and children sometimes clash, and it's good to know when to back off. Occasionally, it is worth getting a tutor, purchasing an online course, or buying curriculum that minimizes parental involvement.

- When possible, get your child's buy-in. However, parents should make the final decision.

There are a variety of ways for people to be educated. Providing the opportunity and resources for our children to learn is more important than the method that is used. Of equal significance is helping our children learn at a pace and in a way that works for them. Rather than trying to match the public school plan, a child should progress as developmentally ready. The public school system is created for the masses, not your child. Pushing too fast or slow will only delay progress in the long run. Each child will excel in some areas, while other academic areas will be more challenging. Consider how you will get the best outcome. Many of us try different approaches and adjust our child's education according to what works. The flexibility to learn at one's own pace is a gift to the homeschooled child. Homeschooling is truly an individualized education for your child.

Homeschooling and Responsibility...

Since homeschooling allows families more time at home and is flexible, it can allow children to be more responsible. This can translate into a good work ethic. When children are home more and less rushed, it is easier for them to take over personal responsibilities. Homeschooled kids have more time to make their bed, feed animals, and make and clean up breakfast. Showers can be juggled, and the kids can tidy up the bathroom and put their laundry in the wash when they are finished. When chores are complete, it's time for schoolwork and a snack. After playing outside for a bit, they can fold their laundry and resume schoolwork. At the end of the day, it is easier to teach personal responsibility when kids are home more.

In addition to helping more at home, over the years, homeschoolers can and should take increasing ownership over their education. A child should accelerate through easier work and take the time needed to understand concepts that are difficult. Likewise, homeschoolers can incorporate areas that schools may overlook or increase their education in areas where they have strong interest. While it is important to follow the law and an educational foundation is a must, ultimately, people need to learn what interests and serves them well.

Independent Homeschool Thinkers...

Families who homeschool think outside the box. We have identified that homeschooling will allow us to raise and educate our children more effectively than we could if our children attended school. By the sheer fact that homeschooled children are not in public schools, they will be exposed to different ideas and will learn to think differently than they would in the school system. When parents choose to homeschool their children, it is clear they believe the benefits of homeschooling outweigh the benefits of attending school. While the reasons parents choose to homeschool their children vary widely, the choice to homeschool is a common thread that can bring us together.

Just as the reasons parents have for homeschooling their children vary, so do the methods for teaching. While homeschool students use a variety of methods and sources to learn, our impression of homeschoolers is incredibly positive. We have noticed that teenagers who have homeschooled their entire lives are frequently avid readers, great conversationalists, and very independent, self-motivated learners. Lifelong homeschooled teenagers frequently expand their own education by following their curiosity. They learn through many sources beyond textbooks, and what is learned sticks because the motivation for learning is intrinsic. The self-motivated homeschooler wants to be competent and knowledgeable. Many homeschool students are voracious readers, excellent writers, creative thinkers, and very effective communicators. Homeschooling creates more opportunity to become very well educated than most people can imagine.

> *"Homeschooling is truly an individualized education for your child."*
> **HOMESCHOOL THINKTANK™**

> "Many homeschool students are voracious readers, excellent writers, creative thinkers, and very effective communicators."
> HOMESCHOOL THINKTANK™

PART III

HOMESCHOOL OPPORTUNITIES

Opportunities abound for homeschoolers. Nearly every community has activities our children can partake in. It is important for homeschool kids to see they are far from alone in this lifestyle. Spending time with other homeschoolers will be beneficial to your family. You will find friendships, information, and a sense of community in homeschool groups and classes.

Here are some ways to find homeschool opportunities. First, check out our website. HomeSchool ThinkTank™ is working to connect homeschool families with one another in a way that works for us! We want to help you *Live & Learn Your Way.*™ Next, an online search with your town's name and the word *homeschool* should pull some results. Also, be sure to check social media for homeschool groups. In addition, your local newspaper and school district may have information. Some school districts offer programs specifically tailored to homeschool students. Beyond that, there are other ways to find homeschoolers. Check with your library, recreation center, local museums, art centers, colleges, and churches. Also, while 4H, American Heritage Girls, and similar groups are open to all children, they tend to draw large numbers of homeschool families. In addition, gymnastics, dance, music, art, and martial arts studios frequently offer homeschool programs during the day.

Homeschoolers are not limited to homeschool activities. You can still enroll your children in local programs that are open to all. Even If a child doesn't attend public school, they can frequently participate in public school extracurricular activities and sports. Also, sometimes you can enroll your child part-time in public school and homeschool the rest of the time. For example, if your child wants to participate in the school orchestra, she might be able to attend orchestra each day, and homeschool for everything else.

If an opportunity doesn't exist that you want for your child, then work to create it. Sometimes, it only takes a few people to get the ball rolling, and new programs can be formed. If the need is there, many will help create programs to serve others. Remember, the mission of HomeSchool ThinkTank™ is to serve homeschool families. Please let us know what your needs are, and we will serve you to the best of our ability.

"Spending time with other homeschoolers will be beneficial to your family. You will find friendships, information, and a sense of community in these groups."

HOMESCHOOL THINKTANK™

THINK HOMESCHOOL.

HomeSchool ThinkTank™ is working to connect homeschool families with each other, the resources, and providers we need. If you know a provider or group who offers homeschool services or activities, please help us connect with them. Visit us as we work to connect you with each other and the resources you need.

GROW WITH US!
www.homeschoolthinktank.com

"When we are intentional about starting each morning, the rest of our day falls into place more easily."
HOMESCHOOL THINKTANK™

THINK HOMESCHOOL

PART IV

HOMESCHOOL ROUTINES

A major benefit to homeschooling is the ability to structure life as we see fit. On one hand, the flexibility of homeschooling makes life easier; on the other hand, life is simplified with a few routines. When we are intentional about starting each morning, the rest of our day falls into place more easily. Here are some basic routines that can help our homeschooling lives run more smoothly.

Longer Blocks…

This routine is based on having longer blocks of time available for very focused learning. This can work well with middle and high school students who have longer attention spans. For approximately an hour and a half *Live Your Way*: eat, do chores, and get outside to move. Afterward, spend approximately two and a half hours to *Learn Your Way*. If a child of any age cannot focus or sit still for approximately two and a half hours, then add a break in the middle of the *Learn Your Way* block. Here is a sample schedule with longer *Learn Your Way* blocks.

7:00 a.m. Wake Up!

7:00 a.m. to 9:00 a.m. Begin with a *Live Your Way* block. Start your morning routine, have breakfast, and get outside and exercise. This is a nice way to jump-start your day. You'll get your blood flowing and mind moving.

9:00 a.m. to 11:30 a.m. This is the morning *Learn Your Way* block. Many homeschoolers focus on core components of education like math and grammar during this time frame. However, some homeschoolers prefer to be active in the morning and save sedentary work for the afternoon.

11:30 a.m. to 1:00 p.m. This is the lunchtime *Live Your Way* block. Have lunch, visit, do a few chores, and get outside for some fresh air.

1:00 p.m. to 3:30 p.m. Afternoon is here, and it's time for another *Learn Your Way* block. Many homeschoolers prefer to do activities like reading, writing, music, and art in the afternoon. Occasionally, this time is needed for appointments or shopping. When it's not necessary to have the kids along for errands, consider scheduling something more productive for them to do. For example, they might have a playdate at a friend's home. Likewise, many parents sign their children up for homeschool classes once or twice a week and run their errands while the kids are engaged in meaningful activities.

3:30 p.m. to 7:00 p.m. *Live & Learn Your Way.*™ Living and learning intermingle heavily during this time frame. Kids might be involved in sports, scouting, theater, or pursue other activities they are passionate about.

THINK HOMESCHOOL

Families shoot hoops, play games, do yard work, and cook dinner together. Homeschoolers don't tend to do much "homework" during this time though!

<u>7:00 p.m. to 9:00 p.m.</u> *Live Your Way.* Now it's time to wind up the day: complete chores, have a family dinner, and get ready for bed.

<u>9:00 p.m.</u> Older children might go to bed somewhere in this time frame. Some kids can't wait to get to bed because it's a nice quiet time to read, write, or draw. Hmm…it isn't "homework," or is it?

Once again, this is an example. Every family has the flexibility to set their own schedule, and you will likely need to adjust for your family. If kids are up late with extracurricular activities and they don't get to bed until 10:00, then push wake-up time to 8:00 and begin your morning accordingly. So long as your children spend time doing what needs to be done, and they are educated, it doesn't hurt to rearrange the schedule.

Shorter Blocks…

Another idea for homeschoolers is to repeat a routine throughout the day. This is especially good for younger kids or children who have difficulty sitting still for long periods of time. Children should do their best during the *Learn Your Way* educational time. Afterward, they'll take a break with a *Live Your Way* block. During this time, children will eat, play, and do a few simple chores. This routine is geared toward younger children who have shorter attention spans and need more frequent meals, movement time, and sleep.

The length of the shorter *Learn Your Way* blocks should match your child's ability to maintain focus and do their academic work in a productive manner. In essence, a six-year-old will have a shorter *Learn*

THINK HOMESCHOOL

Your Way block than a ten-year-old child. Remember to make learning fun by mixing up educational methods and teaching in a way that works for your children. This is so important as we try to nurture our relationship *and* help our children develop a love of learning!

With the shorter *Live & Learn Your Way*™ blocks, figure out how frequently your child needs to eat, and repeat your routine throughout the day around their meal times. Let's say your child eats about every three hours. If meals are at 8:00, 11:00, 2:00, and 5:00, then your schedule would revolve around those times. Your child would have breakfast at 8:00, do schoolwork for as long as their attention span allows, then do a few simple chores and play outside. At 11:00 you would repeat the schedule with lunch, schoolwork, outdoor playtime and possibly quiet time in their room. At 2:00, repeat the schedule again with a snack, some schoolwork and then transition into your late afternoon and evening routine. Around 7:30, cuddle up on the couch for family reading. Younger kids need more sleep than older kids, so with this sample schedule they might go to bed around 8:00.

What's Missing...

Have you noticed an element that is missing to the routine above? It's screen time. We aren't adding pointless television, texting, or gaming into this equation. When we minimize screen time, a lot can be accomplished in a day. We homeschool our children for good reasons; it's likely that creating a couch potato is not something any of us have in mind. The less our children stare at screens, the more likely it is they will develop interests that don't require a power button. Conversely, the more interests a child has, the less they will want to stare at a screen.

THINK HOMESCHOOL

What's Present...

Three components are present in the homeschool routine which are frequently missing in the average American life. The first is time for sleep. We often overlook our own and our children's need for sleep. Sleep is a basic need, and it is our responsibility to ensure our children have the opportunity to get the rest they need each night.

The second component in these routines is time for family. Those *Live Your Way* blocks are bits of time that the family naturally spends together around meals and basic living. Also, as homeschooling parents, we inherently spend time with our kids during the *Learn Your Way* blocks. With time on our side, we have more opportunity to teach, share values, and enjoy our kids. This family time is incredibly important throughout all of our children's years.

The third component homeschoolers have more opportunity for is healthy living. Our homeschool lifestyles are less hurried, and we have more time to prepare healthy meals and snacks at home. Also, we have more time to exercise. However, healthy living doesn't just happen. As parents, we must lead the way by stocking the kitchen with nutritious food. We should also provide the opportunity for our families to get outside and move. Fresh air and sunshine will help improve our family's mental and physical health. When we immerse ourselves in open, nature-filled spaces, our families will be happier. Ultimately, homeschooling is conducive to raising children in a healthy manner. As leaders of our families, we must take the steps to raise healthy children.

HomeSchool ThinkTank™
• live & learn your way •

"Ultimately, homeschooling is conducive to raising a family in a healthy manner. As leaders of our families, we must take the steps to raise healthy children."

HOMESCHOOL THINKTANK™

PART V

HOMESCHOOL HURDLES

School isn't perfect, and neither is homeschooling. However, many homeschoolers would agree that challenges associated with the public school system are far greater than hurdles associated with homeschooling. Here are some common problems homeschoolers face and some ideas on how to deal with them.

Financial Challenges...

For some parents, the first challenge to homeschooling is dropping one income. If you've been a two-income family, this can seem daunting. However, there are a myriad of ways to cut costs so one parent can stay home with the kids. Maybe you will consider the following ideas to reduce household expenses.

THINK HOMESCHOOL.

- Refrain from adding more to life. Each time we add another mouth to feed (pet or human), an additional loan, a bigger home, another activity, and more stuff, we create more expenses.

- Look for ways to shave monthly bills. Can you live in a less expensive home? Can you drive a more affordable or fuel-efficient vehicle? Many of us can reduce our cable bill, phone bill, and other subscription services.

- Trim the grocery budget. Consider reducing unnecessary expenses, like junk food, when shopping. Have you thought of stocking up on frequently used items when they are on sale?

- Reduce dining out expenses. Perhaps you can split meals when dining out. Maybe everyone can drink water instead of soda. Take a snack bag and water bottles along for errands.

- Reduce clothing expenses by purchasing items when they are on clearance or on sale. Consider finding a good thrift store. Many costs can be drastically reduced, and you might be surprised at the unique and useful items found.

- Have you evaluated other activities and their associated costs? For example, signing up for a sport is only the first step. There are usually additional expenses like uniforms, gas, dining out, and possibly hotels.

As we consider our expenses, we want to keep the activities that will bring long-term gain while eliminating those which are simply taking our time and money without great benefit. The key is to evaluate whether the financial and time cost of an activity or item is benefiting the participant proportionally. Hopefully, these ideas can help you reduce your expenses so one parent can stay home. However, there may still be other options if this is not feasible.

Work and Homeschooling…

For families who want to homeschool but need or want to keep two incomes, there are other options. Some homeschool families may be willing to educate other children alongside their own. Also, family members who don't work outside the home may be willing to help with homeschooling a child. Finally, consider hiring a tutor. This could be a retired teacher or another individual who is trustworthy, knowledgeable, and good with kids. Ultimately though, as parents, we are responsible for our children's education.

For some, it might be possible to work from home. For people who have computer-based jobs, this may be an option. If this isn't feasible, could you bring your child to work a few hours a day? For example, older kids can bring their schoolwork in the morning, and you could enroll your kids in an afternoon homeschool program. There are many variables to consider, as this certainly won't work for everyone.

Finally, each family knows their situation best. However, if you wish to homeschool your children, we encourage you to find a way. Be creative and search for a path to make it happen. Homeschooling is not just a gift to your child; it is a gift to your family.

"Homeschooling is not just a gift to your child; it is a gift to your family."
HOMESCHOOL THINKTANK™

THINK HOMESCHOOL

The Expense of Homeschooling...

Families who want to homeschool are sometimes concerned about the expense; this is not difficult to overcome. Homeschooling can be as expensive or inexpensive as we make it. By utilizing our public libraries, we can reduce the cost of homeschooling drastically. Books, documentaries, computers, games, and entire courses can be found under the library roof. Also, with an online search, we can quickly find an abundance of used curriculum for sale. Thrift stores and used bookstores are also good places to look. In addition, many homeschool families exchange, sell, or give away their books when they are finished with them. Finally, when you want new books, there are many affordable curriculum sources available in bookstores, online, and as e-books.

Homeschooling With Disabilities...

Sometimes children have disabilities, and sometimes a parent has a disability. Disabilities range from mild to debilitating. If you have a disability, only you can decide what is best in your situation. Likewise, there are numerous concerns you will need to consider if you want to homeschool your child with special needs.

- How severe is your child's disability?

- Can you receive services in your home?

- Can you receive services through the public school system? Do you want those services?

- Do you qualify for grants designed for homeschool families who have children with disabilities?

THINK HOMESCHOOL

- Will you need to hire outside help for housekeeping, shopping, and yard work? Even the most dedicated parents have limited hours in the day. Depending on the severity of your child's disability, you may need help.

- How many other children do you have? How old are your children?

- Who can serve your child best? You, the public school system, or another entity?

- How can you help your child receive the most suitable services?

If your child's disabilities are severe, you will likely need help in some form. However, if your child's limitations are minor, can you educate yourself on how to best serve your child? Please visit our website to add or find links that might be helpful to parents who are homeschooling a child with special needs.

Time Alone...

For many of us who are stay-at-home parents, it can be a challenge to find time to be alone. With some foresight and planning though, we can overcome this hurdle. The easiest way to achieve this is by enrolling our children in either homeschool or after-school activities. Another way is to swap kids with another homeschool parent on a regular basis. The kids can have educational or play time together with their friends while you have a few hours to run errands or relax. This could be done in the home, at a children's museum, park, or even the recreation center. Another option for finding time to be alone is to ask close family and friends for help. If you ask, many people have a hobby or skill they might be willing to share with your children. Finally, your spouse and kids can probably find something meaningful to do while you get a break. Sometimes we need to be home alone for a while, and sometimes we need out of the house. Either way, it's nice to have some time apart, and it's good for the kids to spend time with other people who care about them.

Another challenge is for everyone to have daily time to themselves. Consider building a routine that includes quiet time. Children can learn to appreciate an hour alone in their bedroom. When kids don't have their own room, help them find a space where they can be apart from their siblings. This is a great time to leave electronics behind and encourage children to entertain themselves. They can read, write, draw, play Legos, or play a solo game like solitaire with a real deck of cards. Quiet time can bring peace in the home when we need it most.

> *"Quiet time can bring peace in the home when we need it most."*
> **HOMESCHOOL THINKTANK™**

Children also need time alone with each parent occasionally. Kids are more likely to open up and share what's on their mind when it's just the two of you. So, whether you stay up late visiting with one child after the others go to bed or go do something fun, make an effort to have one-on-one time with each child periodically.

Last but not least, if you are married, take care of your marriage. It is all too easy for us to spend all our time and energy on the kids. However, your marriage is your family's foundation. Your spouse deserves your attention, and your kids deserve happily married parents and an intact family. Take the time and make the effort to nurture your marriage. Your children will thank you for it later.

THINK HOMESCHOOL

Parent and Teacher...

There are effective ways to be both parent and teacher. The first is to create routine in the home. When we create routine, we minimize nagging. Life is easier when everyone knows what to expect each day. The second suggestion is to have a planner and chore book for each child. Discuss each day's plan, and your child can write what needs to be completed. Keep track of curriculum and educational activities in the planner and chores in a notebook. As the day proceeds, you will think of tasks the kids need to do or notice things they forgot to do. When possible, instead of interrupting your child while they are focused on something else or overlooking what they forgot, add the chore to their list. A chore book will reduce your need to repeat yourself. As a result, you will have a better relationship with your child.

The final step to being both parent and teacher is to quietly be consistent. While we can adjust chores and schoolwork as needed, there should be a baseline that is expected each day or week. When children complete their work, then they get to do the things they look forward to. When they don't meet realistic expectations, then we get a break from taxi-driving, and the kids can stay home and do what they should have done in the first place.

> *"When children complete their work, then they get to do the things they look forward to."*
> **HOMESCHOOL THINKTANK™**

THINK HOMESCHOOL

Keeping the Routine...

For many parents, the greatest challenge to homeschooling isn't creating the routine; it's keeping the routine. There will always be something or someone to interrupt our plans. While distractions are inevitable, many are not urgent. Attempt to make a conscious decision about what truly needs to be done now, and what can wait.

One common way to disrupt the school routine while helping the kids is with phone calls and texts. Clearly, there are times when we must take a call or respond to a message. However, recognize that each time we disrupt the school day, our children lose powerful momentum and precious time. Consider proactive measures like setting your phone to Do Not Disturb during *Learn Your Way* blocks. In addition, let others who are likely to call or stop by know ahead of time that you are unavailable during certain hours.

If it is difficult to stay focused at home, consider going to the library or somewhere where it is easier to stay on track. Regardless of how and where homeschooling takes place, by setting boundaries ahead of time, the potential to homeschool successfully is increased.

Finally, running basic errands can be a challenge for homeschooling parents. Plan ahead and schedule appointments and shopping when your children are involved in other educational or meaningful activities. Visit our website for more ideas about time management.

> *"...recognize that each time we disrupt the school day, our children lose powerful momentum and precious time."*
> **HOMESCHOOL THINKTANK™**

THINK HOMESCHOOL

PART VI

HOMESCHOOL LAWS AND MORE

In this section, it is not our intent to provide legal advice. Our objective is to provide basic information and help the reader find additional, reliable, easy to understand information about laws that govern homeschooling. Neither the author nor HomeSchool ThinkTank™, LLC is qualified to give legal advice. This segment is written with an American audience in mind.

The first step to homeschooling is knowing the law, and state laws vary widely. Generally speaking, you will want to follow the law of the state where you live. However, there may be exceptions to this rule. An excellent organization that can help you understand homeschool requirements is Home School Legal Defense Association. For more information on specific state laws, visit HSLDA's webpage.

THINK HOMESCHOOL.

You might also be wondering, "Who can homeschool their kids?" One way to find out is to go to your State Department of Education website. In many states though, a parent with a high school diploma can homeschool their children. Your State Department of Education website should line out what your family will need to do should you choose to homeschool your kids. If your children have been in school, be sure to disenroll them from the school system, or the school may consider your child to be truant. As you contemplate homeschooling, there are many considerations to take into account. Home School Legal Defense Association is a valuable resource that can help you understand your responsibilities as a homeschool family.

High School...

While it is an option to take a G.E.D. test, homeschool students can earn a high school diploma. Begin learning what is required for a high school diploma by checking with your State Department of Education and Home School Legal Defense Association. Another option to earn a high school diploma is to enroll in an online high school program. However, whether publicly or privately funded, be sure to research any program you enroll your child in, as online high schools vary widely. Finally, many homeschoolers have begun taking advantage of dual-credit programs offered at local colleges. These programs allow students to earn a high school diploma while simultaneously earning college credit. For detailed information, check with college personnel.

Throughout the high school years, it is important to prepare for and take tests that are frequently used for college admittance and more. Consider taking standardized tests, such as the Iowa Test of Basic Skills, at least once a year. In addition, begin preparing for the ACT and SAT. Understand that your child is likely to do better each time the test is taken. By understanding how the test is structured and what to expect, your high school student will be better prepared to perform at a higher level. Please see our website for more information about testing.

College...

College-bound homeschoolers should begin reaching out to colleges of interest as early as possible. With each college, inquire about what will be needed from a homeschool student and what additional steps can be taken to stand out in the application or scholarship process. Your teenager can be better equipped to enter college by having an early understanding of what is expected. Many colleges offer services with homeschool students in mind and are more than happy to help your student navigate their way to college.

Trade Schools and Vocational Schools...

Maybe your child isn't interested in earning a traditional college degree. If your high school student has a passion and college isn't of interest, then a trade school might be the answer. Follow the same steps you would for college. Find out what's expected, apply for scholarships, and start creating a plan and developing skills to help achieve that goal.

No College or Vocational School...

While college or vocational school can be a good path toward career and financial success in life, it is not the only path. If your child can earn scholarships for school, then financial concerns are few. However, if you or your child is paying for that education, or if student loans will be utilized, then it pays to weigh the costs against the benefits of either college or a vocational school. If a degree is necessary for a career, then higher education is the only way to achieve that goal. However, for many careers, a degree is unnecessary, and there may be a more

THINK HOMESCHOOL

efficient way to achieve the same result. Sometimes, parents and teens are so focused on college, that we don't stop to think if it is the best path to take. Remember to weigh both the time and financial cost of a degree against the benefits of that degree. It is worthwhile to consider the outcome we want in life and the best way to get there. Often, there are a variety of paths one could take.

If higher education is not in your child's future, you still need a plan. Help your high school student find something they are interested in, and start building skills now. Find someone who has the needed skills to mentor your teenager. As your child enters adulthood, a mentor can be a valuable guide.

While we understand that college is not the only way to go, it is important for homeschool students to be prepared for college if they choose that road. So stay diligent, and make sure your child is prepared for college even if they don't think that's the route they will take. As teenagers enter adulthood, it is important to keep as many doors open as possible. Regardless of the path your child wants to take, help create a plan that will lead toward success and financial independence in life.

> *"It is worthwhile to consider the outcome we want in life and the best way to get there. Often, there are a variety of paths one could take."*
> **HOMESCHOOL THINKTANK™**

PART VII

HOMESCHOOL HOPEFULLY

Homeschooling is a fantastic opportunity and should be a parental right. Thankfully, in the United States, we have the right to homeschool our children. We are grateful for organizations who protect our homeschooling freedoms. In some countries, parents have been stripped of the right to educate their own children.

We have been conditioned to send our children to school, so most of us don't initially consider homeschooling as an educational option. Many don't realize we have the right to homeschool our own kids. Just as it was natural for our great-great-great grandmothers to be stay-at-home mothers and even teach their own children, it has become natural for our society to hand children over to public institutions. At the age of five, nearly all kids attend public school, so this seems normal. For

THINK HOMESCHOOL

some, staying home with their children is something that hasn't been considered. Hopefully, we can help change that. Parents can be the best and most loving teachers a child will ever have. Children deserve and need time with family. Homeschooling nurtures these bonds.

For most of us, there is a catalyst which brings homeschooling to mind. An event happens we don't like, and we begin wondering if there is a better way. The answer is, "Yes, there is a better way."

If you have decided to homeschool your children, "Congratulations!" This road is not always easy, but it is worthwhile. Homeschooling can improve family life, our children's lives, and their education and future in ways that we cannot yet foresee. When we homeschool our children, we must sow the seeds, and the entire family will reap the rewards. From years of experience and observations, we have learned a great deal. May we offer some suggestions?

- Have confidence in the decision to homeschool. We should be kind, but firm, in this decision. There will be naysayers. However, the more resolve we have, the less we will be questioned. This is a personal, family decision. While we want to be polite, we do not have to explain ourselves to anybody. The simplest statement is, "We've decided to homeschool the kids; it's the right decision for our family." We should expand only with the people we want to share with.

- Remember, we are the parents, and we make the decisions. While we may have asked for input from older kids and had family discussions, parents decide what will be best for each child and the family. The more we waffle, the more difficult it will be for our children to transition from school life to homeschooling. Even when kids want to homeschool, they may

THINK HOMESCHOOL

have a hard time transitioning. Most people don't like change–but don't worry–homeschooling will become the new normal.

- Create special moments and experiences that relate to homeschooling. There will likely be something the kids miss about school, but always have an event to look forward to that can only be done because they homeschool.

- Connect quickly with other homeschoolers. There are lots of homeschoolers in the world, and our children need to know they are not the only homeschooled children on the planet. Join homeschool groups and classes created for homeschoolers. Many homeschool groups have park days and take field trips together. When we are part of these groups, we receive the emotional support we need, useful information, and build close friendships.

- Build daily shake-ups into the routine. Consider being consistent with core curriculum time, but make each day a little different from the one before it. For example, Monday includes a music lesson and a playdate. Tuesday is gymnastics. Wednesday meet friends at the park. Thursday, go to the library. Friday, plan a homeschool field trip. The weekend is a combination of chores, fun, family time, and downtime.

- Add one subject area at a time. Get one thing going smoothly, then add another subject. Start with the most important core areas like reading, writing, and math.

- Consider year-round homeschooling; the advantages are huge. This can happen in many different forms but can make homeschooling more enjoyable. By spreading schoolwork throughout the entire

THINK HOMESCHOOL

year, we reduce stress and increase academic retention. While we can lighten the load in the summer, our children will continue to progress with academic skills. In addition, the transition into the following school year will be much smoother.

- If you choose to homeschool year-round, schedule breaks throughout the school year. Depending on the number of hours spent on academic curriculum each day, you might schedule 20 to 60 weekdays off over the course of the year. Consider overlapping some breaks with the public school schedule. This makes it easier for kids to play with their school friends occasionally.

- If your children have been in public school, do not jump into full time, year-round homeschooling at the beginning of summer break. Give the kids a couple weeks off, but limit screen time. When screen time is limited, children are encouraged to entertain themselves in more meaningful ways.

- Consider beginning homeschooling in the following manner. Start with daily reading. Also, children should keep a journal, as this encourages enjoyable writing. Next, add board games like Yahtzee® and Monopoly®. Make learning fun. Begin by making education more fun than work. To reduce your chance of strong resistance, ease into curriculum one subject at a time.

- Remember that instilling the love of learning is more important than any curriculum.

- Finally, we must nurture relationships with our children. Teaching our kids should not be a battle. When what we are doing is not working, then it's time to find another way.

THINK HOMESCHOOL

We hope you have decided to homeschool your children. This lifestyle can allow your family to grow and thrive together. Clearly, you care enough and are smart enough to find the resources you need to educate your own kids. Concerned parents who read this book will certainly take the necessary steps to homeschool successfully. In the age of the internet, the world is at our fingertips. Nearly everything you need can be found with your next online search. Be flexible, but persistent, and you will succeed.

HomeSchool ThinkTank™ connects homeschool families with one another and the resources we need.

Scan This Code!

GROW WITH US!
www.homeschoolthinktank.com

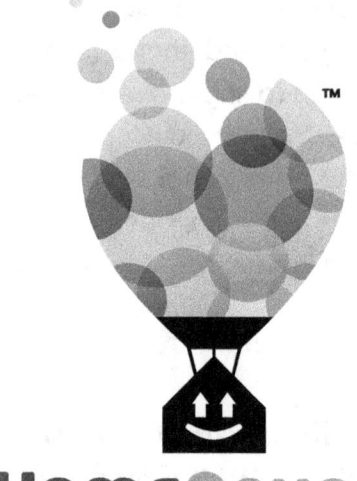

HomeSchool ThinkTank™
• live & learn your way™ •

GROW WITH US!
www.homeschoolthinktank.com

HomeSchool ThinkTank™ connects homeschool families with one another and the resources we need.

PART VIII

ENCOURAGING EPILOGUE

Whether you homeschool your children or not, raising children well takes dedication and perseverance. While we begin by wanting to create a family of our own, it doesn't take long to realize what an incredibly long-term commitment rearing children is. While we know this going into parenthood, it is difficult to appreciate that fact until we are in the midst of parenting. While our kids will live with us for the first eighteen years or so, they will forever be our children. We want our kids–young or old–to lead fulfilling, happy, meaningful, and successful lives. We want this for them, and we want it for our own peace of mind as well. As parents, we want to know we have done everything in our power to help our children succeed.

THINK HOMESCHOOL

When our kids move out, we should feel we have done a fine job raising them. While we guide them through academic materials, there are other areas of life that are equally, if not more important. We want our children to have strong values, good relationship skills, and the knowledge and confidence to create the life they desire. We want our adult children to have morals that push them to give more to the world than they have ever taken.

May each of us have the courage, the patience, and the flexibility to do what is best for each of our children. When we put one foot in front of the other each day and wear a smile more often than not, we can change our family's life for the better. Homeschooling is a lifestyle that can serve a family well. Is this the right decision for your family? Only you can decide what is best for your children and family. If homeschooling is right for you, may you feel empowered to homeschool your children and *Live & Learn Your Way.*™

Best Wishes,
HomeSchool ThinkTank™
Live & Learn Your Way™

"Parents can be the best and most loving teachers a child will ever have."
HOMESCHOOL THINKTANK™

THINK HOMESCHOOL

Do you want to know how homeschoolers make friends?
https://homeschoolthinktank.com/10-ways-homeschoolers-make-friends/

GROW WITH US!
www.homeschoolthinktank.com

HomeSchool ThinkTank™ connects homeschool families with one another and the resources we need.

GROW WITH US!
www.homeschoolthinktank.com

HomeSchool ThinkTank™ connects homeschool families with one another and the resources we need.

THINK HOMESCHOOL©
• live & learn your way™ •

NOTABLE ACKNOWLEDGEMENTS

Thank you to my beloved husband. Without your constant support and encouragement, I could not be the wife, mother, or woman that I am. You are steadfast and the foundation of our family. I am grateful every day that I married the right man, the first time. I am fortunate to have you for my husband. I am grateful for the decades of love we have shared. Our daughters have no idea how lucky they are to have you as their father. You make our lives amazing.

Thank you to my daughters. I am inspired by you. You both have gifts to bring to this world. Dad and I want to help you bring *your* dreams to life. We are blessed to have you as our children. Each of you are cherished and loved as the unique human beings you are. We love you and are proud of each of you.

THINK HOMESCHOOL

Monica Woodward, of iDesign, you have been instrumental in bringing both HomeSchool ThinkTank™ and *THINK HOMESCHOOL*© to life. Your design shines light on my vision. You have delivered more than I could imagine with both the HomeSchool ThinkTank™ logo and *THINK HOMESCHOOL*© cover. Thank you for your foresight, patience, encouragement, intelligence, and creativity.

David, my brother, I am ever so grateful for your unending patience, support, and guidance with all things computer related. Thank you for your support and encouragement as I launch all parts of HomeSchool ThinkTank.™ It touches me deeply.

To that special mom who asked about homeschooling; your question inspired my answer. While the reason behind the question is heartbreaking, I hope the answer will be helpful to all who consider homeschooling. I wish you and your family the best as you begin the homeschool journey.

Amy & Jeff Pierson, thank you both. Amy, I cherish our 30-year friendship. Thank you for the guidance and referrals to the people who can help bring *THINK HOMESCHOOL*© and HomeSchool ThinkTank™ to life. Jeff, thank you for taking photos for this book and my website. Also, I thank you for taking so many family photos over the years. Your photography work is outstanding.

Mandy Walters, thank you for spending a day with me taking photos. I will forever cherish that day of fun and laughter. I am delighted with the back cover photo. I am so glad we took those final shots!

THINK HOMESCHOOL

To my family, extended family, and friends. Thank you for listening to all my excitement as I brought *THINK HOMESCHOOL*© and HomeSchool ThinkTank™ to the world. I appreciate your unending encouragement and support. I hope you have more of that in store, as the HomeSchool ThinkTank™ story is just beginning!

JACKIE WHEELER
Founder

HomeSchool ThinkTank™ connects homeschool families with one another and the resources we need.

THINK HOMESCHOOL

ABOUT THE AUTHOR

Copyright Jeffrey Pierson Studio 2018

Most importantly, Jackie Wheeler is a wife and mother. She believes strongly that family is important, and parents are the most influential teacher a child will ever have. Jackie's family is incredibly important and dear to her. Ultimately, nearly everything she does in life is about and for her family.

Jackie is also the founder and owner of HomeSchool ThinkTank™, a company formed to help serve and support the homeschool community. HomeSchool ThinkTank™ connects parents and children with the information, motivation, and resources homeschool families need.

Jackie holds a Bachelor of Science in Physical Education and has taught P.E. in both a private and public elementary school. She has also taught in a nationally accredited preschool. While Jackie enjoys a variety of hobbies and activities, currently her life revolves around her family and HomeSchool ThinkTank™.

Jackie Wheeler lives in the Southwest among the mountains and mesas with her husband, two daughters, and a myriad of animals. Jackie enjoys the multitude of benefits and pathways for growth that homeschooling allows her family.

GROW WITH US!
www.homeschoolthinktank.com

THINK HOMESCHOOL

HOMESCHOOL THINKTANK™ HAPPENINGS!

HomeSchool ThinkTank™ was born out of necessity, determination, and a strong desire to share information about homeschooling. We connect homeschool families with one another and the information, motivation, and resources homeschool families need.

We are committed to serving homeschoolers and collaborating with others for the good of homeschool families. Our website and services will be growing week by week, month by month, and year by year. We are so excited to serve homeschoolers! We invite both homeschoolers and those who serve homeschool families to connect with us.

WE HAVE A BIG VISION!
CHECK IN AS WE CONTINUE TO GROW!

• live & learn your way™ •

GROW WITH US!
www.homeschoolthinktank.com

GROW WITH US!
www.homeschoolthinktank.com

HomeSchool ThinkTank™ connects homeschool families with one another and the resources we need.

www.ingramcontent.com/pod-product-compliance
Lightning Source LLC
Chambersburg PA
CBHW052206110526
44591CB00012B/2102